WE HAVE ALL BEEN

Broken

BEN REKITTKE

Contents

Afterlife

Plop.
Such an odd useless word.
A sound surrounding an event
when water meets it's Mother for the first time.
Plop.
There it is again, I wonder if the
rhythm will remain. Yep.
Plop
Down here we are all equal.
Down here we are not brothers,
just taller walled in scavenging vengance.
Why do we want to live?
Just lay down
and let death brush across your
face and take a soul.
Then we get to enter the afterlife.
Eternity sounds much worse than life.
Heaven is a lie.
We love to tell ourselves
that when we die we will be happy.
Death is a gift

Amused

If only there were more vodka this
minute would fuck itself into
Oblivion
Into a 360 madman cackle that
leaves spectators Amused,
Bewildered,
Entertained,
Burdened by irrelevant evidence.
This one minute.
It had meaning.
It possessed grace and dignity.
This one minute held my attention for eternity

Anger Gets A Hug

Anger is my love
My comfort place
my mother
My sweet perfect place that can't kill me
Anger is energy
IT MUST KEEP MOVING.
It can be changed into positive energy
This is what your brain was built for
To alter your violent instincts
Just take a deep breath, allow your mind to
communicate with your anger
Exhale and you will know anger is controlling you.
Do you want to be controlled by anger?
No you don't.
Anger is an emotion that has the ability to control
your actions, in the act of identifying anger your
conscious self may control your
instinct of violence.
Therefore you are in control
Of anger
Please do not read this.

Angry God

Anger
I hate you
Not in the natural way
but in the seething complicated slow poison
that devours souls and morality
in such a way that it slams its boot on Gods neck
and turns faith into theatre.
God was once angry
I miss that God.

Anger

Anger
You sweet bastard cupcake fucking angel
I love you
You lurk
You sleep
You nap
You care
I see you slinking around the room
waiting to murder reason
Screams, accusations, untruths made true
Face bashing, rib fucking mayhem
All the cute stuff
Anger you hideous bastard
I love you
You nailed my face
to a gas station bathroom door
Anger is the weak enemy
The next fight is
Greed.

Are you the Devil?

I walked into a bar,
it looked like Davey's in midtown KCMO
I saw a man coveting a beer and was intrigued.
He was sitting at one of the high round tables.
I sat next to him.
He turned his face slowly as if
scanning the room and revealed

his black hole eyes and angular face
that was burned beyond reparation
of some past that was now awakening.

I knew I was dreaming,
I have seen him before
so I asked
Are you the Devil
Yes he replied
He must be the opening act.

Art

Poetry you cunt
You useless object worshipped by 22-77 people
has become the cigarette doors and bearded dogs
Screeching for the new blank grey world.
None of that means shit, it's not
poetry wrapped in a poem,
Like a fetus in an egg
Mimeless blind alternative bands
that launch generic cunt poetry like this
Destroys art
This poem hates art
THIS POEM HATES ART
This poem loves you

Baby Hot Baby

What I love has nothing to do with you
Broken conversations
Dirt
Loud discarded men
Smiles from children
Children are the unfiltered, untamed,
little perfect humans shot out of
Excited vaginas.
Squishy boneless babies
$7.99/pound

Baby Slice

I delivered a human baby in a dream last night
It began walking within seconds
of being shot out of a machine that one would
normally purchase a coke
I didn't help or deliver this baby actually but
she did tell me a story (all covered in blood, I
cut her HDMI cable with my Swiss army knife)
"I am here to educate you on the
aspects of imperfect human"
99% of Humans are arrogant, selfish, power
seeking, unethical, greed driven sluts that would
sell their own mothers flesh for a pound of love
Who are you?

Ball-Mart

Lit?
No
I'm that quick slow-motion passion burn
that just turns into an old man
waiting to die in line before it's his turn
Tons of sex,
a trip to Columbia,
a rock-star tease,
a near death experience that
was nowhere near death,
ocean, despair, happiness, aids-candles,
gay gambling
Dolphin-fucking weekend
not really it was a Tuesday

Ball-Mart Exploded
A peaceful expression sprinted across God's face

Bee

Walking Bee, a sixty-five pound dog,
in a large field I looked up
and became the black sky bellow me
Orion was stretched out over the sky
as if attempting to kick the moon
in an Aztec Tlachtli Game.
I stopped,
as if at an alter in an impossible church.
A space so vast and full of life
my belief in God sent me a chilled warmth
A tingling sensation you feel when you know
how complicated the universe is
and how your tiny life
Actually means something.
All life has meaning
There is no plan.

Birth

We are brutally shoved into this
world from our Mother.
The life conduit cut, (our first separation)
we cry and need and cry and
cling and seek warmth
from our Mother
The Mother loves more than
she will ever love again.
This little human she has made.
This little human that she will love
and teach and scold and reward
This little human will write his own story
through his deeds on your heart

Black Friday

Why are you talking
Everything you are asking about is gone
Do you need to purchase
something to make you feel
better about yourself?
If I buy this for my husband he won't
mind if I gave Jeremy, my 10 year old
sons best friend, Carlos, a hand job in
the Burger King men's room will he?
I'm NOT DRUNK CRAIG
CRAIG
CRAIG YOU FUCKING WHORE
STOP, STOP, STOP
SHUT THE FUCK UP
FUCK YOU SHANNON,
Fuck no fuck you Craig
"Hello my name is Ben how can I help you"
Ben I need to talk to god
Hold please…
God is down at the moment
I can connect you to Allah
Or perhaps you would like to talk to Kali
"YES KALI WOULD BE AWESOME"
Connecting you to Kali, I must
place you on on a brief hold

Blackout Sex

Blackout sex

Blank White Bastard

You blank white bastard why should I paint
a love story on your face
"You need me"
You need me, without me you
would just be wrapping up
a trout or some bloody beef.
"I was invented to record the history of humans"
Humans can be ego driven
creative when it comes to
recording history.
"There is no such thing as recorded history"

Boba Fett

With new wounds and perplexing
bruises I drive to work.
I enter the box and begin to do my job....
I sell things to people who don't need
things and then I sell them accessories' to
things they will never need and sometimes
I love them, too much...........
Sometimes I open tiny frightened eyes
to the magic of digital everything.
"Can you make this" YES I CAN
Can I add words"
YES IT'S CALLED TYPE IN THE PRINT INDUSTRY
THAT IS
CHOKING ON IT'S OWN FAILURE
DUE TO A DYING
revolution.
Um.....ok cool can I just add
"Happy new year from
the Sinfucks",
Arthur, Jill, Abby, and Max(lol Max is the dog)
YES
YES I CAN
SHUTUP AND LICK MY BOBA FETT
ACTION FIGURE FROM 1981
BITCH

Body Machine

Some people want, need to be someone else
They want to be special,
unique, talented, skinny and pretty
The most terrifying thing is endurance
the vicious pain of endurance
We only have one soul and a
current body machine and 9 billion dreams
God is a complicated comedian

Break Your Fathers Heart

Break your Fathers heart
drink his last beer
become familiar with his future
He lived in a world of dust and next door TV
fields of corn and tomato's and chasing bee's
My Fathers father was a steelworker
and enjoyed an organic garden, advised
against adding salt to meals, a forward thinker,
he dreamed while watching that
silky sunset steel melt,
only to see it shaped into destruction.
He kept bee's, that's how he would teach his sons
responsibility to catch them,
and control them before
he got home
–Mary

Build

Build a fire
Invite a stranger
Build a house
Invite a family
Build a street
Invite twelve families to build houses
Build a well
Build a hospital
This is a fill in the blanks test for you humans

Buzzard

No light.......
I am on my back.
Old house dusty invasion smell
like grandfather cockroach graves.
Breathing in is nothing
compared to the taste of breathing out.
I can move my legs, and roll a bit.
I am shackled at each hand and ankle
with about 3 inches of slack
laughing at my inability to escape.
Fuck you mind,
I will win this day
Fuck you finger monitor.
Fuck you midnight nurses and hollow interns
that would rather staple me down
than knock me out.
O this story
I was thrown out of the Buzzard beach
from the front door to the street
30 feet below
Good street broken glass times
I was tied down
as if I was a lunatic in the hospital

Thank you
for restraining me
I would have killed
all of you

Carolyn

I have never met you Aunt Carolyn
but I miss you
I have missed you
all my life
I have only heard stories
and attempted to reconstruct
a relationship with you
I miss you
I have met your children
I have met your sister
but still I wish to meet You.
I miss you

Cashews

It would take 870 years
to reach Neptune but it is an ice planet,
I have a cryo-pod ready
to launch you there if you like.
Why do I have a cryo-pod?
I predicted that someday
cashews would become extinct
So I invented a way to prevent that
with cryogenics

Need A Brand New Chainsaw

Machine sell me some noise
and God play with your toys
I hear the dog that cries
I'm to weak to die
Need a brand new chainsaw
need a place to fall
need a brand new chainsaw
like to kill us all
The rain crawls over me
The walls following me
The rain crawls over me
The walls following me
Need a brand new chainsaw
need a place to fall
need a brand new chainsaw
like to kill you all
You think you are dead
it's all in your head
you think you're alive
you think you're alive
need a brand new chainsaw
need a place to fall
need a brand new chainsaw
like to kill us all

When the Circle met the Square

One fine sunny-cloudy day
the Circle was floating
across a shapeless space
towards nothing
and was met by the square.
The square was startled and said
"Hello, what are you?
"I am circle"
"how can you live without corners"? square said.
"Are corners those ugly bends in
your body"? said Circle
"The bent parts are called angle's" said the Square
"Why do I not possess such angle's"
said the circle I am not ready

Clitcam

There is a tiny camera
in Lady Gaga's cyborg clitoris.
It will control your TV
and mannequin servants

Clowns

Poetry lies
It hates you
It makes you read it,
Knowing you will enter
a new world
That is a lie
Although lies are just other worlds
telling the truth
Hmmmmmm the truth
Humans are so obsessed
with the truth they need
Lies to make the truth appear righteous
Something never talked about
Clowns fuck gas stations sandwiches
just to stay alive

Common Fence

Common sense
is a safe and useless explanation
for someone whom did not share
your entire life experience.
A man from Kansas City, Missouri
has no common sense in New Guinea.
A man from New Guinea
has no common sense in Kansas City, Missouri
The man from Kansas City
would be dead within 3 days.
The man from a culture
that has not changed since the stone age
would be interesting, and interviewed,
examined, sampled, probed
and then returned to his home.
He would die with stories
laced with exploration poison.
Leave them alone.

Cricket

This tower of wine thinks
it can best me at a game of cricket Ok so
Ok
Wait um ok

It's baseball with an ass-beating paddle,
you "throw" a "ball" and then a man hit's it
and runs somewhere?

For fuck sake I don't care

The best part is that the
"Greatest American Pastime"
is BASEBALL

It's called rounder's by the English

Yes our greatest American sport
was invented by the English
Thank you King George Bush the stupid.

Peace

A crowbar solves every problem

Cursive

Cursive is an outdated form of
writing that is usually illegible.
It was invented for taking notes 100 years ago.
The disconnected 26 letters of our
(Greek/Phoenician) alphabet
is just fine for taking short notes
and much more legible
to the note taker.

Finding points on a line of text
and using them correctly
is much more
beneficial
Stop.

Czar

She rubbed her small
brown belly and shot a sigh to her boss
"So can you let Tina go home"
"yeah, it's a bit slow and Andrea comes in at 8"
An hour earlier she double dog
dared me to take a shot of moonshine
I did, and liked it cranberry style
This is a true story but
I kinda feel bad about putting
"cranberry style" in your head.
But hey at least
I did it twice

Death on a Hot Plate

Love slips delicate
Between beauty dragged
underneath oblivion into an
unknown impossible place,
and a useless blurry dry mouth morning
I know why we kill ourselves.
I know why logic
makes everything reasonable
And "best for everyone"
I know why we kill ourselves
It's like walking out of a bad movie
that just won't shut up

Deep Unyielding

Seventeen green faces painted blue shove
bloodshot angry eyes at
me while the bus bumps and rattles
through the streets of the
unwanted.
There is a deep unsleeping grey
mass in their hearts.
There is a deep unyielding day that starts
To wait
To middle
To no end
To stumbling south of reason unspoken.
So I sit
relaxed
daydreaming.
Why must I be the test subject on the slide.
My midnight was scheduled to die
while my tomorrow was
keenly broken.
That bastard fly-fishing sun
nearly caught me
So close and so slow
So sweet and so kind
I knew at that moment
it would never be
Mine.

Desecration

IT'S A BLOODY MESS
ANGER
INSULTS
DESECRATION
OF FORGOTTEN THOUGHTS
I HATE YOU
I hate you
Tell me lies and
PAINT MY FACE

Dolphins

Superman glides into his apartment on the plaza,
picks up the purple phone
to order a super strong ass sausage
and holy Jesus prawn pizza when
Suddenly
A carved from something
carved temptress breaks down
the door with her
Carved ass back hoe (damn)
SOMETIMES DOLPHINS CRY

Dreamkiller

Burn your dreams to the ground
Resurrect them
Break them into a billion pieces
Remake them stronger
Kick that dream killing beast in the face and
Demand your destiny.

Each Day

Each day given
saves a lie for tomorrow

Easter

Poetry requires combat
with the drones
The drones coffee down
the predetermined path
to the dull little loading dock
that deposits them into a square
thought killing occupation.
It's kinda like painting
with honey based blood laced
with dead end job opportunities'
and the Easter bunny
The fucking Easter bunny
scares the fuck out of me
with his giant fangs
and rape list
Those scorpion ears
that will kill you……
slowly

Evolution

Humans have been attempting
to control the masses through religion
and laws for thousands of years
Anyone happen to notice
this approach at control
NEVER works.
Does the threat of the death penalty
matter to someone willing to murder?
NO.
Does the fact that some drugs are illegal
EVER STOP ANYONE FROM TAKING THEM?
NO.
I am not an anarchist,
I am just living in an age of human evolution
that appears to have stopped evolving completely.
We should only need a government
to provide services for the population.
Instead we have "representatives"
that control our destiny.
The only crime to carry a sentence
of death should be Greed.
Odd
I hate being a sensitive person,
it allows me to see the destruction of evolution in
human beings.
We have not created a better place.
We have NOT EVOLVED.
Extermination recommended.

Fancy Fuck You

I hate the word Fancy
I do however love the word Shmancy
but how can I use the word
Shmancy without Fancy?

Die in a starving car fire

Farmer

Bone breaking work
Taste the land
Read the wind
Bless the rain
You are a farmer
"I will break your nose
and jam it up your ass"
"why" she said
"I need to go write
but all I want to do
is break your nose and
Shove it up your ass
until I find that place
where it stops Dieing.
It should just click into place
like a Kodak printer cartridge
She is screaming more than usual,
I shove a sock full of chimp feces
into her mouth and what do I get
MUFFLED DRAMA based on nothing
anyone ever wants to listen to

Find Chris Wolfe

Vengeance
Super magic
Non-aggressive,
bitch-slapping
Ego
Power
Soft woman skin
Tall
Pride
Hollow cock
fantastic fantasies
Power
Clutch a single glorious moment
and hold on
HOLD ON
Wait
Piss down these dead walls
and beat the lifeless life from them

Frank

A lobotomy bouncy house
with all the squishy stupid parts of people
would be a delightful addition
to my quiet close friends
who prefer to stand.
"nothing crazy for my birthday"
Thanks,
Frank
Friday
All prophets are false.
Predicting the future is impossible.
Can anyone think of any prophecy
that we have avoided by listening to a prophet?
No, we cannot.
We are spinning on a rock in space at
40,000 miles per hour around a star
1,000,000 times the size of that rock.
The ego and vanity of humans is offensive to me.
Greed is repulsive and useless.
IF we manage to not destroy ourselves
I would love to see the results of our Evolution.
Presently we are not evolving much at all,
and at times I think I am part
of a social experiment that involves
"The study of primitive bipeds,
and why they love themselves and not each other"

Box

Why do I hate you?
Does hating you heal my pain?
No
You did not create my pain,
you are just the lucky cashier
that gets to ring me up.
I make so little money
that I am subsidised by my government.
ALL AMERICAN TAXPAYERS
ARE PAYING 7-8 MILLION DOLLARS EACH YEAR
TO PART TIME WORKERS IN THE US
IF THESE LARGE CORPORATIONS
PAID THEIR EMPLOYEES
JUST A LITTLE BIT MORE
YOUR TAXES WOULD NOT GO TO FOOD
STAMPS AND UNEMPLOYMENT.

Fire

Damn you poetry
Damn your pretty face, Tuesday Damn
you black days and blind nights

The Concept of Choice

HUMANS DO NOT CHOOSE TO BE GAY
FOR A CHOICE TO BE VALID
THERE MUST BE AT LEAST TWO
OPTIONS. DO I CHOOSE TO BE GAY,
OR DO I CHOOSE TO BE NOT GAY.

Fish

This wheel
It turns and finds ways
to shout lies
It turns
It thinks
it turns
It hates and yet smiles
without cause or reason
It turns and thinks
and begins to dive
SPLASH into an ocean
of horrible poetry
A place escapable
A common horrible place
made of words and feelings and
Useless faith that this poem
may have been
Interesting.
God loves gay fish.

Freedom

Obviously some humans
with limited intellect will be barbaric, ignorant,
closed-minded and useless
when a debate involves Homosexuals.
The King James version of the bible
is not included in the Constitution of
the United States of America.
We have the freedom of religion and
the freedom FROM religion

Gladius

O, the rest of you?
That's fine
I wasn't thinking either.
Help you?
Yes please and thank you
(didn't do anything yet, you may want to hate me)
My daughter wedding baby shower reunion aunt
who has passed away
I just want to sometimes things are so….. clear
and the children are so precious cat food
sometimes I love to dance…..
O look there is Arthur,
and me in 193..194.…1947.
I just love pictures
They..
Freeze the past and let us cry in the future
Can you help me
Yes

The Recycled Arena

Generation still born
Stillborn revolution
Stillborn Tuesday
Stillborn legacy
Stillborn shout
Stillborn observation
A stillborn observation
100 stillborn observations
100 pomes left to die
Lost on dark bridges
Whores and Ice cream trucks
Stillborn whores who hate Republicans
Stillborn whores:
The congress that does not represent the people
Stillborn whores:
you are 1% WE ARE THE 99%
90 % of Americans want to legalize Marijuana
for recreational use.
Kinda thought the USA was a democracy.
Maybe there is some sort of magic funtime glitter
Republicans use to sprinkle on there balls at night

Moonshine

"You are born with dreams crushed by
God" "Then what is my purpose in life"
the human asked
"To rebuild your crushed dreams
and make them better, and stronger"
God has compassion for the loser

Nut

If I'ts ok if that your gay 19 year old son
holds up a republican convenience store
and steals some beef jerky and cashews
I demand to be created by my 6000 year old
planet God earth Jesus science truth distortion
wow that is a puked pome that I cant explain

Painting Eyeballs

Poetry hates republicans
It is the only generalized hate
that exists with poets
I hate poets
That's what they call us anyway
Poets
All this anti-individuality
is why we are unable to evolve
Human beings were created
to evolve independently.
Not at the cost of family,
or social interaction, or collaboration.
If God wanted a stagnant world
that never changed we would not be here today.
God wants to observe evolution,
otherwise he would have just created a painting
Human beings will always write poetry.
Just read the bible.
It was written by Human beings
God just nodded off reading chapter 3

Gold

Human's are thousands of years behind
most what we would call "Animals"
Humans created the concept of
the wealthy and the poor.
Humans created the middle class.
Humans created the value of needs
represented by little sheets of paper.
Humans have decided there is value in gold,
and diamonds.
Why
Gray
Art and Music programs
are being cut all over the United States
from public schools.
In two generations the United States
will be populated by a few thousand republicans
Who finally got their silence
and gray dead walls painted……..gray.
There is no soundtrack as music
has been labelled useless

Greed Pride Vanity

Yes we humans are animals
that have created a distorted sense of morality,
religion and justification of genocide.
We believe we are the most important aspect
of evolution in the past 12,000 years.
There are many species
that lived long before we "evolved"
and they will live long after our relentless ego
destroys all life on the planet earth.
Human beings will for the first time in our earth's
history
destroy all life on this planet by choice.
Evolution decided to exclude greed,
Pride and vanity as they are unnatural
and the seed of our destruction.
Humans created all three

Greed

When a shithead becomes a
CEO of a large company
does it actually care about anything?
No. If this shithead fucks up
he will be paid 10 million dollars to get fired.
Yes the CEO is an it,
and doesn't care about anything or anyone.
Buy the way this poem is 12000 years old.
Greed is is the greatest of all sins
If anyone named Noah is reading this,
please welcome the lions to the plush,
useless kings of oppression.

Compassion

Ah yes the warm helping hand of healthcare.
Fuck the useless poor drones
Thank you so much for burying me in mass graves
during useless wars.
Haditha

Hope

I handed God a picture
and a description of women
her name is Hope
The eyes the psycho-volcanic eyes
destroy fascination
beyound the dream
The eyes
penetrate me with nails and warmth
I would slide down a mountain of razors
for a glimpse of her shadow.

Ice Cream

True love is useless
It waits in a corner
Like a pro
Waiting not needing
hating and needing and faking and
SHAKING YOUR FATED little eyes to
TURN WHITE AND FORGIVE ME.
Fuck it
Lets get Ice cream

Prison

It's a friendly place
until you want to leave.
That's when you get shot in the face.

Julia

Cold.
Exposed hands, and feet.
Burning wrists and ankles
in a tight rough ziptie grip.
Dark. So tight
I am in a nothing space room
and my hands are broken
against my broken feet.
Mouth stuffed with something.
A disgusting old man stench
belt strapped tightly around my mouth.
A light under a clean door flicks on.
Two hammering dirty bootsteps
stride from the light to my confinement
SMASH the door is splintered
"Hello Julia, my name is Nathan"
"MY NAME IS NOT JULIA!"

Popbots

Miley Cyrus
she knows what things mean, like
a wheel or crab rangoon

Justin bieber is the new pinup girl for 1946

Libby

The smile caught me first.
The soft sharp eyes
full of clowns and angels.
The hips
The eyes
The flip-flopped feet that decided
to rest upon the back of the chair in front of us
like she owned the place
Beauty has a new name

Lillyskin

Living on antifreeze
in my world I can't be seen
emptiness walks across to me
but I won't open up
Take it away
every day
love your pain
underground is where I like to breathe
suffocate in violence
wrapped around
inside your walls
breathing in your silence
Take it away
every day
love your pain
I see a dream
it's out of focus
so delicate
and fearless
Stained glass
eyes
Black and white
Take it away
every day
love your pain
Lillyskin

Lincoln

Why are there Republicans and Democrats?
We should not have either,
our elected members of congress
should vote as individuals not as a mob.
Systems of communications
have improved since the late 18th century
We no longer need the senate
or the house of representatives.
All campaign contributions
from any corporation should be abolished
Only individual contributions
should be accepted and made public
The newest cold war
is between the Democrats and the Republicans

"A house divided against itself cannot stand."
-Abraham Lincoln

We the people should all be
allowed to vote on everything.
Like a fucking senator
getting a raise for no reason.

Live

Pouring fast feet into faster legs
for a boss that hates themselves
more than reason
I sprint to shine headlights and shoes
and destryod needs and dreams.
This is why we have all been broken,
this is why we survive

Mouth Hole

A musician should be challenged
by performing live at every show.
A lip sync is not a performance,
your just a pathetic mouth hole.

My Illustrated Life

Missouri.
you hot wet cotton bastard of August.
I love you.
The single slow churning overhead fan
moves the heat from corner to middle,
only to repeat it's useless path over and over.
Jack Patel-Goldstein reaches for infinity
and slams to the floor.
Keeping an important tight grasp
on the last of the bottle of Johnny Walker Black.
Jack pours the rest of the once
loved bottle into his mouth,
spilling most of it on the floor,
Cranks both triggers on his replica road warrior
double barrel shotgun at what appears to be
Jorge Ortiz-Epstein, Sommelier

Just Admit It

You voted for Obama
because he's black

CHAPTER 1

Observations And Nightmares

Old man suit sox
Cool its raining
Shut the fuck up
You're dog loves me
It's raining shut the fuck up
Sometimes humans think
SHUT THE FUCK UP
I'm taking B for a walk
Ok

Olivia

Hello Olivia,
You are amazing, cool, beautiful,
intelligent, and talented.
These are your genetic gifts
from your Father and Mother. Music,
athletics, mathematics,
or anything else you would like to do.
You are an individual.
What you want to do is your choice
but whatever you decide,
everything listed above will help you
on your way. Don't be like me.

Paralyzed

See me out there
why do you stare
I hide my eyes
breath in my lies
My pastel crimes
paint pantamimes
burn pleasently
inside the sea
I feel so paralyzed
My window crawls
trapped by my walls
drain me of light
imortal night
I feel so paralyzed
Don't hesitate
to hang your mate
I hung myself
just to improve my health
I feel so paralyzed
I feel so paralyzed
I feel so paralyzed
never will I see a brighter day

Women Are The Makers

Women
Women are the illusion
The sanctuary
The gatekeepers of madness
The soft goodbye
The kiss
The 9mm solution to an illdisguised problem
The reason why unreasonable has a name
Women are the makers
Of all of us
If only Women could alter the genetics
of every offspring to produce
Males who possess the drive and ambition
for space exploration, science,
philosophy, and art. Instead of
EGO DRIVEN RAPISTS THAT NEVER THINK

Words

Poetry
is the invisible knife
Sharp fast useful
forgotten

Pride

Pride is the death of reason in disguise

Purpose Haiku

Murder my shoeface
Murder my perfect treason
Murder my purpose

Smoking. . .

On the wet green porch swing
Half dreaming I'm in a park
In 1979
Wet green porch swing
Sideway windy rain devouring a cautious wind
Smoking again
Laughing
Running to and from
misplaced love
Just stop and shut the fuck up
.... looking,
judging, waiting, needing Stopping, stopping
Anything with an end in its agenda destroys you
To much thinking leads to misguided
Motivation
take a walk in the rain

Rat

The ugliest woman alive
boarded the green west worley bus at 9:45
am I was still a bit drunk from the night before
She began to screech like an entitled rat
at the bus driver as if he were a servant
The bus driver wanted to stab her
So did I
she just continued screaching
surely she thought her elevated status
would make the bus go faster
The bus driver and I continued to stab her
She continued to screach without words
and the green bus kept crawling
along it's predeter- mined path,
and the rat kept screaming along her path
both destinations
meaningless.

Sane

148 pounds of darkness
Vs.
A thimble full of sunshine
Sometimes it's best to let your subconscious
drive you home

Boss

Fuck you
Fuck your dead racoon slackjaw
salem cigarette breath.
Obviously you are an idiot.
You speak like a puppet
and clearly have never had one creative thought
either enter your tiny broken mind
or been excited by one.
You are a disgusting use of matter.
Your voice is hell slicing evil for a
sad sandwich Satan
"Would care not to Shit on or devour"
Please just stop talking
Forever.

Slip The Hook

I spent
many
nights with
blue smoke
dead thighs
black eyes
kill your
philosophy
nothing left to
fuck or
kill

So Long

I let it out of its cage
it had to think of things to say
it needs to crash
and find its mask
and stop reaching
for the beginning
It takes so long
Search and locate its bright face
recollection of disgrace
it needs to land
in my hand so
I can smash
i'ts last breath
It takes so long
I'm so excited I can finaly smile
mysun is setting somewhere else
I let you into my disguise
I lift up my tired why's
So long
drag my face along

70

The young
So many mental fantasy fun thoughts
6-10 years old
We should manufacture every idea
from a 6-10 year old perspective
I Ben Rekittke, 43 believe my ideas
were cool at 6 (1978)
but it was the 70's and most stuff in the 70's
was fuelled by cocaine and Steve Jobs

CHAPTER 2

Songs

We will control you
Stop writing
Words just don't suit you
Why would you write a book?
Your blank stare could fill a warehouse
with idiot symbols of flying machines
and human thinkers
Shut the fuck up
you sinister little thinker.
We hate you
We will stop you.
We hate thinking.
STOP THINKING
We love you, (purrrrr)
We will control you
We know what is best for you

The Damn Goodbye

You told me once that I was incapable
of a mature long term relationship.
You said that if I didn't know what was wrong
you would not tell me.
You told me that I didnt want you enough.
You didn't want me either
and this leads me to the point
of why I am sending this to you
Love is a useless concept for you,
it means nothing to you.
Being in love with someone means
nothing Stop calling me.

The Dream

Spit me out
into the cold hand of Gods lost children
out here I am the anti human soul
such perfect work you have done
tiny razors rip-rake my guts
Tear them out and fling them into heaven or hell.
The splatter of useless chatter
fills my ears with flies
Shut up
staple your stench laden lips
together and scream no more
I am inside looking down deeper
than the lowest murmur
beneath the dream waiting.

This Eclipse

See sparrow crash
on scattered wings
and all it lacks is spiraling
Now I know why
the candle learns to glow
by method acting
out your bad dreams
And so the greys
stare down through me
as Art Bell dreams
the spy learns
spine will tingle
i can't mingle
my own thoughts with
every single
cell that can't sink
can't swim can't all outside

this truth remains a lie
Terror in the sky
So I see
where we live
we all fall down
through this eclipse
Now I know why
the candle learns to glow
by method acting
out your bad dreams
Statutory wine
slipping down the vine
inhaling you deepest dark trials
I am only you staring back through me
colliding with what we desire
Penetrate the lies
terror in the sky

Tic Toc

I don't want to write
I don't want to sleep
I don't want to think
I don't want to smoke

eat

drink

fuck

scream

kill

create

shit

vomit

spit out the voice that tells me to stop
I don't want to live
I don't want to die
I don'want the end
I don't want the birth
The clock beats
ignoring my complaints.

Time

Insanity has it's place,
a place humans have discovered
but have yet to express
as a pure life
color
a
complicated state of decisions
that don't exist

Treason

Stop

Think

Words

Pain

Love

Need Stuff and things

that would make me Happy

Satisfied

Terrified

Lost in a long dead tribe of reason

Lost in a drowning sense of Hope

Treason Understanding

Misunderstanding Dead love and perfect stars

We walk And think And become

what we need to be.

Tweenpires

Hey True Blood,
Hey Twilight

STOP WHAT YOU ARE DOING YOU ARE MAKING
VAMPIRES HAVE FEELINGS THEY HATE FEELINGS
AND WISH TO KEEP FEEDING ON THE INNOCENT
–MANAGEMENT

Truth 47

SURPRISE!
US troops leave Iraq after 13 years of "War"
and chaos with a splash of religious insanity
rapes the middle east.
War over religion within Islam
has lasted 1400 years.
Shia and Sunni Love Allah (God)
Israel and Palestine
both love God
All middle eastern
Jewish and Christian religions
love the same god
What the fuck

Truth Mule

Trapped and captued I find the
beauty of the stars
and the Zoroastrian ritual of cleansing
section download
Magi nods a beaten reason
to take a step into the fire
truth is a whisper
shouted faster than light

Vagina Blanket

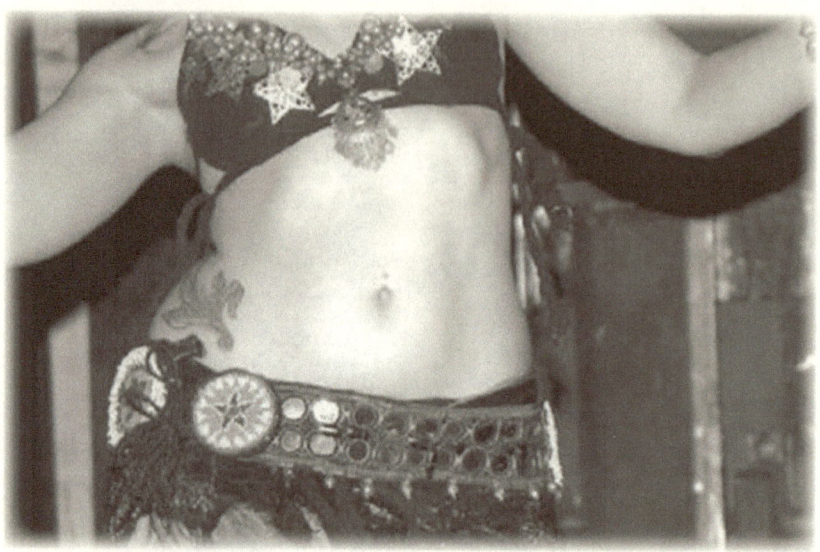

Surrounded by the warm vagina of my blankets
I find it futile to attempt escape.
The pure heroin warmth is irreplaceable;
there is no feeling like this in all of human sensory
perceptions.
I count from 39 to zero thinking
I will launch victorious from this soft slipping flesh
but each time I get to 39 I smile and start all over.
Counting coming going dreaming killing painting
walking flying hating curling.

Wet Black Night

The wet black night covers me
in non-conversation.
Exterminate,
make love to and beat the emo kids
into a less interesting version of me.
Pulverize us all into a black shit mash of anger.
Pride is the ugly side of progress.
I am the strongest man alive

Wine 42

Failure
Magic sweet failure
I'm out of wine
O wait ....
there you go
now I'm out of wine
Hello, my name is the beginning of odd tales
to be forgotten and found
and burned and studied
like a razor uncut.

Women Are The Makers

Women
Women are the illusion
The sanctuary
The gatekeepers of madness
The soft goodbye
The kiss
The 9mm solution to an illdisguised problem
The reason why unreasonable has a name
Women are the makers
Of all of us
If only Women could alter the genetics
of every offspring to produce
Males who posses the drive and ambition
for space exploration, science, philosophy, and art.
Instead of EGO DRIVEN RAPISTS
THAT NEVER THINK

My Love

You left me the day we met